WORKING WHEELS

Bulldozer

Annabel Savery

W
FRANKLIN WATTS
LONDON·SYDNEY

First published in 2009 by
Franklin Watts
338 Euston Road
London NW1 3BH

Franklin Watts Australia
Level 17/207 Kent Street
Sydney NSW 2000

ISBN: 978 0 7496 9291 9

Dewey classification number: 629.2'24

A CIP catalogue record for this book is available
from the British Library.

Planning and production by Discovery Books Limited
Managing editor: Rachel Tisdale
Editor: Annabel Savery
Designer: Ian Winton

Acknowledgements: Alamy: p. 19 (qaphotos.com); Deere: pp. 12, 17, 24; Dressta: pp. 5, 9, 13 top, 15 inset, 21; Getty Images: p. 27 (Neil Massey); Istockphoto.com: cover main (Julio de la Higuera Rodrigo), pp. 7, 16; Komatsu: title page & pp. 4, 6, 15, 28, 29; New Holland: cover top right, pp. 14, 25; Shutterstock: cover top left & p. 23 bottom (Sergei Butorin), pp. 8 top (Alexey Fyodorov), 8 bottom (Chris Hellyar), 10 (Koer), 11 (Tom Oliveira), 13 inset (Chris Hellyar), 18 (Robert J. Beyers II), 22 (Lloyd Paulson), 23 top (Ron Hilton), 26 (Jose Gil), 30 (David Touchtone); Terex: p. 20.

Printed in China

Franklin Watts is a division of Hachette Children's Books, an Hachette UK company.
www.hachette.co.uk

Contents

...t are bulldozers?

...rs are powerful earth-moving machines.
...can push vast loads.

As a big bulldozer drives along, anything in front
of it is collected by the **blade**. Bulldozers can
move earth, rubble or rocks from one
place to another.

Crawler tracks

Blade

Bulldozers have strong **crawler tracks**. With
these they can travel over rocky ground or
soft, sandy ground without getting stuck.

Big bulldozers are used to do some of the toughest jobs. They work in all sorts of places, including mines and **landfill sites.**

Bulldozer fact!
Some bulldozers are so powerful that they can move trees, or even a house.

Parts of a bulldozer

Bulldozers are used all over the world. They come in many shapes and sizes. Look at all the parts on a bulldozer. Do you know what they are all for?

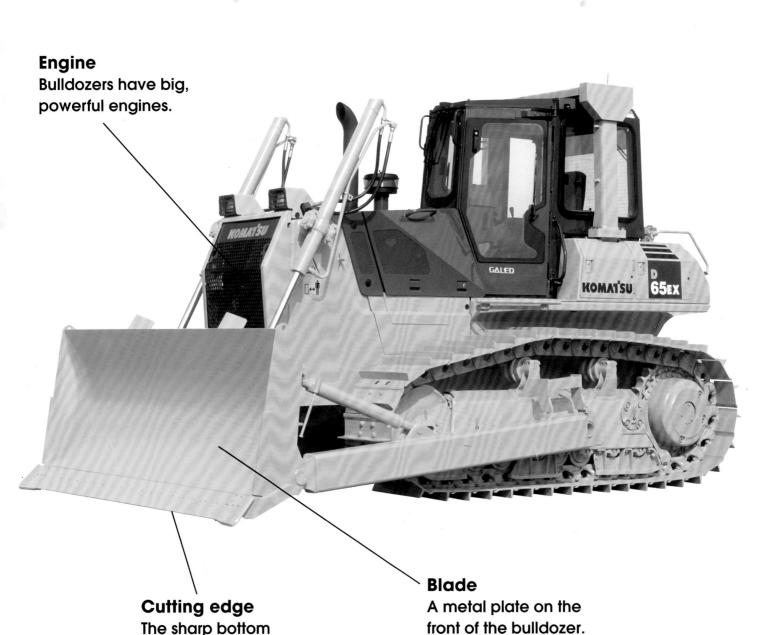

Engine
Bulldozers have big, powerful engines.

Cutting edge
The sharp bottom edge of the blade.

Blade
A metal plate on the front of the bulldozer.

Bulldozer fact!

Some bulldozers are over four-and-a-half metres tall — that's the same height as a double-decker bus.

Cab

The **operator** sits in the cab to control the bulldozer.

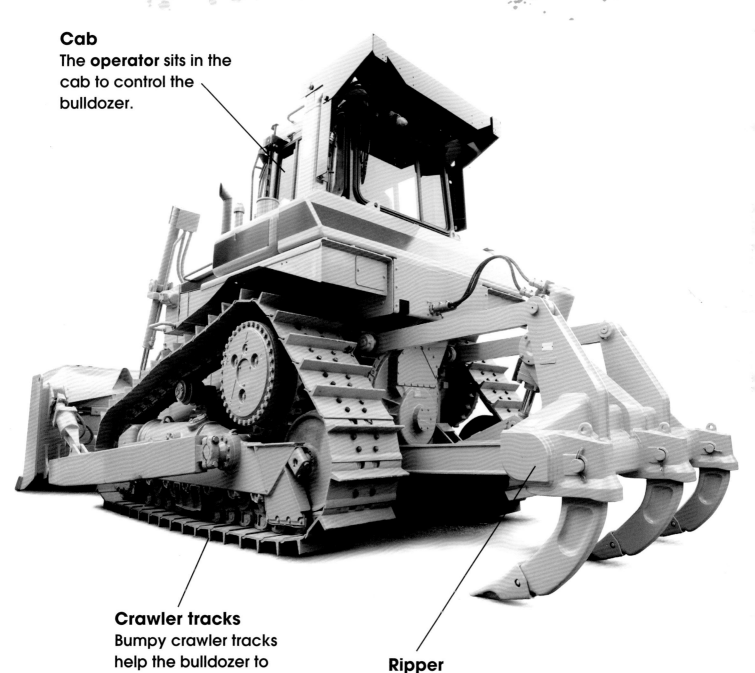

Crawler tracks

Bumpy crawler tracks help the bulldozer to travel over any kind of ground.

Ripper

A tool that is used to break up hard ground.

crawler tracks

Most bulldozers move around on crawler tracks. These are tough belts made of metal. They are stretched around two wheels.

Crawler tracks

The tough belts are made of lots of sections joined together. These sections are called **shoes**. The shoes have bumps on them.

As the bulldozer moves over soft ground, the bumps on the shoes dig into the surface. This stops the bulldozer from slipping.

Shoes

Crawler tracks are very strong and will not break on rough, rocky ground.

Crawler tracks are wide and long. The bulldozer's weight is spread out over them, so it does not sink into soft ground.

Bulldozer fact!
Some crawler tracks are six metres long.

The blade

The blade is probably the most important part on a bulldozer. It is made from a very tough kind of metal called **steel**.

The blade is fixed to two arms that can move up and down. The operator can control how high or low to have the blade.

Arm

Blade

Cutting edge

The bottom of the blade is called the **cutting edge**. It is sharp and can cut through lumps of earth.

There are three main types of blade.
There is a flat blade, a curved blade
with curved edges, and one
that is inbetween the two.

Bulldozer fact!
The biggest blade is
taller than an adult.

The ripper

Bulldozers can break up hard ground using a ripper.

The ripper is attached to the back of the bulldozer. It has a strong metal **shank** that looks like a big claw.

Shank

The operator lowers the ripper so that the shank digs into the ground. As the bulldozer moves along, the shank is pulled through the hard ground. This breaks up the ground.

Bulldozer fact!
The shank has a very strong tip. This is separate and can be replaced when it gets worn out.

12

The loose earth can then be scraped into a pile by the bulldozer blade.

Some rippers have just one shank. Others can have two or more shanks. These are known as **multi-shank rippers**. These bulldozers (above and left) have three.

The cab and the engine

Inside the cab there are driving controls. The operator can control the engine and move the bulldozer around.

There are also controls for the blade and the ripper. The operator can move the blade and ripper up and down. The blade can also tilt from side to side.

The cab has big windows all around, so that the operator can see out clearly.

Engine

Engine

A bulldozer needs a very powerful engine. It must make enough power to move the bulldozer and push any **material** in front of it. The engine uses **fuel**, just like a car engine.

Bulldozer fact!

The biggest bulldozer uses over 1,600 litres of fuel in one day – that's the same as 800 family-sized bottles of fizzy drink.

Pushing power

A bulldozer's main job is to clear areas of land.

The bulldozer operator drives through the area that needs to be cleared. Any loose material piles up in front of the blade, and a clear path is left behind it.

If the operator has the blade just above the ground, anything on top of the ground will be pushed along.

If the blade is lower down it will dig into the ground. As it moves along it will remove any lumps of earth and make the ground surface level.

Bulldozer fact!
The largest bulldozer can push 220,000 kilograms – that's the same weight as 220,000 pineapples.

At the construction site

Bulldozers are used at **construction sites**.
They work in a team with other big machines.

When buildings are knocked
down, all the old materials are
scattered on the ground as
rubble. The bulldozer is
used to clear the site.

Bulldozer fact!
Big bulldozers can weigh
over 104,000 kilograms
– that's more than ten
adult elephants.

The bulldozer moves the rubble into a big pile with its blade. Then a digger can scoop up the pile and a truck can take the rubble away.

The bulldozer makes the ground surface flat again so that new building can begin.

Other jobs for bulldozers

Powerful bulldozers are also used at landfill sites and in forests.

When a rubbish truck empties rubbish into a landfill site, it falls in a big heap. The bulldozer spreads out the rubbish so that it fills the landfill site evenly.

As the bulldozer drives over the rubbish it squashes it so that it takes up less space.

In the forest, big bulldozers are used to make roads and move **timber**. They can travel easily over the rough, uneven ground.

The powerful bulldozer can clear small trees and shrubs away to make a path for a road into the forest.

Bulldozer fact!
Special bulldozers are used to help put out big **wildfires**. They scrape trenches into the ground so that the fire cannot spread.

Snow ploughs

Snow ploughs help out when it snows.
They work in a similar way to bulldozers.

Most vehicles cannot drive in thick snow, so a
snow plough is used to clear the roads. Snow
ploughs have a bulldozer blade attached to
the front.

As they drive along the road they push the snow
along too, leaving the road behind them clear.

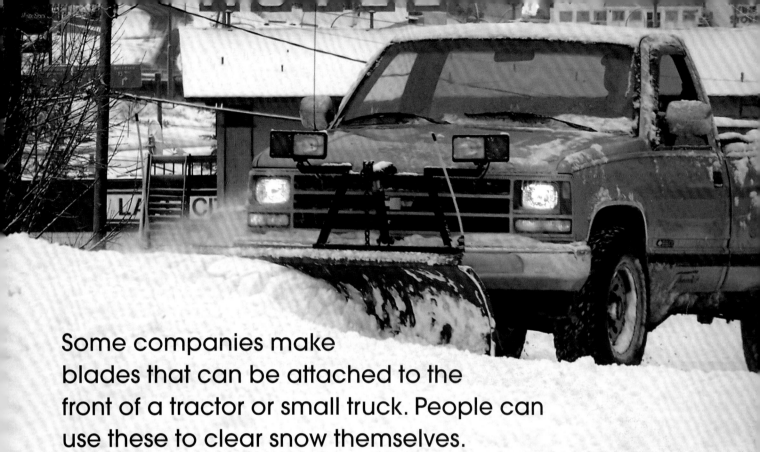

Some companies make blades that can be attached to the front of a tractor or small truck. People can use these to clear snow themselves.

Snow plough fact!

Another type of snow clearing machine is called a snow blower – this cuts through snow and shoots it out of a funnel.

Small bulldozers

Big bulldozers can only be used where there is lots of space. In smaller spaces, such as gardens and building sites, smaller bulldozers are used.

Small bulldozers are much lighter than big bulldozers. They have smaller engines and are less powerful. But even though they look small, they can still move a large amount of earth.

Small bulldozers have a blade and crawler tracks, just like big bulldozers do. But they don't have rippers.

Some small bulldozers do not have cabs with doors and windows. Instead, they just have a frame that the operator sits inside.

Bulldozer fact!
Small bulldozers are sometimes called calf-dozers.

The biggest bulldozers

The biggest bulldozers are used in the toughest jobs. They are used in mines and quarries to move tonnes of rock and earth.

One of the biggest bulldozers cannot travel on the roads. It is so heavy that it would break up the road surface. Instead several trucks move pieces of the bulldozer, then it is put together at a building site.

The biggest bulldozers can move almost anything. They can be nearly five metres tall and can weigh more than 13 adult elephants.

Bulldozer fact!
The biggest bulldozer creates the amount of power as 1,150 horses.

Spe- ial bulldo-ers

Some bulldozers have been changed so that they can be used for particular jobs.

This bulldozer has been adapted so that it can destroy **anti-personnel landmines**.

Anti-personnel landmines are devices that explode if they are stepped on.

A demining bulldozer has a wheel at the front instead of a blade. As it drives over the ground the anti-personnel landmines explode underneath it. These bulldozers are so strong that they are not damaged by the blast.

The cab is made from very strong metal and glass. This means that the operator is protected from the explosions.

Bulldozer Activities

Geography: In which countries do bulldozers do the most mining?

History: What do you think people used for pushing jobs before bulldozers were invented?

Science: What do you think is harder for a bulldozer to push – sand or rocks?

Literacy: What do you think it would be like to be a bulldozer operator? Write a short story about being a bulldozer operator.

Design & Technology: Design and make a model of your own special bulldozer. What job will it be able to do?

Glossary

anti-personnel landmine a device that explodes if it is stepped on or driven over

blade the metal plate on the front of a bulldozer

construction site an area where something is being built

crawler track a metal belt that is stretched around two wheels. It helps vehicles travel over rough ground

cutting edge the sharp bottom edge of a blade

fuel liquid used to power a vehicle's engine

landfill site a large hole in the ground where rubbish is buried

multi-shank ripper a ripper that has more than one shank

operator the person who drives the bulldozer

ripper a device with a strong metal shank that is used to break up hard surfaces

shank a sharp metal point on a ripper

shoe a section of a crawler track

steel a type of hard metal

timber cut wood

Further information

Bulldozers (Big Machines), David and Penny Glover, Franklin Watts, 2008.

Diggers and Cranes (Usborne Big Machines), Caroline Young, Usborne Publishing Ltd., 2006.

On the Building Site (Machines Rule!), Steve Parker, Franklin Watts, 2008.

Index